STEALTH CA

THE ESSENT

C000052009

LUKE VANDENBERG

2nd Edition

Nothing behind me,
everything ahead of me,
as is ever so on the road
- Jack Kerouac, On the Road

Published 2017 by Altiora Publications

AltioraPublications.com

Copyright © Luke Vandenberg, 2011, 2017

Altiora

Acknowledgement
The author gratefully acknowledges the contribution of **Dr David Tuffley** and **Altiora Publications**, for Part 2 of this book, namely the

1

excerpt from his book *Being Alone.*

CONTENTS

PART 1: STEALTH VAN LIVING

This is a primer for anyone looking for information on how to setup a stealth camper van and live comfortably, safely and economically in a typical urban or suburban environment.

There are plenty of reasons why you want to make a home in your vehicle. It might be to enjoy the freedom of the road, or perhaps you cannot afford to pay rent, or don't want to. Perhaps you don't trust the government and want to fly under their radar. Or maybe you are working to save money and want to live close to where you work.

Whether through choice, or through hard times, living in a stealth van can be a good way to go – but only if you go about it right.

It shows you how to live so as not to be noticed by the law or others, making no problems for anyone and minding your own business.

Most communities have anti-vagrancy laws, but as long as you stay unnoticed and don't create problems, stealth camping is usually tolerated by law enforcement. They have bigger problems to worry about than you not paying rent.

THE VAN – HIDING IN PLAIN SIGHT

Stealth campervans hide in plain sight, so it needs to blend into the urban environment. It *must* not look like a regular campervan in any way. No curtained windows, external gas bottles or souvenir stickers.

The best kind is a commercial van that looks like a tradesman's work vehicle. Look at what kind of vans are most common in the environment where you will operate, and choose one like that.

Notice in how many tradesmen's vans there are on the roads. They are everywhere; people rarely give them a second look.

The North Americans, Europeans and the Japanese have been making generic-looking commercial vans since the 1970's, and have been exporting them to the world. Being working vehicles, they are heavy duty and reliable, cheap to buy, run and repair. Most get reasonable fuel economy.

Vans like this are spacious enough for you and your gear but not so tall that they cannot fit into multi-story car-parks or other confined spaces. Any van will be a compromise, but the kind described here is about the optimum compromise for the single-handed stealth camper (or plus one very good friend).

VAN EXTERIOR

White is a good colour, being the default colour for commercial vans, perhaps because it is highly visible and makes a ready background on which business names and logos can be displayed. Black might look cool and stealthy, but ironically, for a stealth camper, it draws attention to itself. You might be mistaken for a police surveillance van, or worse, be run into by someone who does not see you until too late.

Quiet motor. Its an obvious advantage to have a vehicle that starts and runs quietly. If you keep it at low revs, the neighbours will barely notice.

Roof racks that are permanently fixed to the vehicle reinforce the tradesman's van look. On the racks, an extension ladder and even an optional six inch diameter PVC tube running the length of the vehicle, the kind used by electricians to store conduit, completes the look. The ladder should be locked securely into place to prevent theft, and the conduit-holder can be empty.

Signage on the van indicates more than anything that this is a commercial vehicle. It is not strictly necessary to have *any* signage. You might opt for the completely clean look. If you *do* decide to use signage to help you blend in more effectively, it should be something generic-sounding, like *Ace Electrical Contractors*. It's a good idea to have a working cell-phone number with voicemail in the name on the van setup. Also, an optional URL for a basic website also in the same name. Law enforcement or curious others might well call the number or visit the website to see if this van is what it says it is. These precautions will usually be enough for them to leave you alone.

It will confirm that this is a commercial vehicle belonging to a business, and will allow you to stay overnight in loading zones and other areas reserved for commercial vehicles.

No light escapes the van interior at night. Being window-less is a good start. This leaves the opening into the driver's compartment and the rear windows to make light-proof. Many vans have a steel mesh partition just behind the driver's seat. You can keep this in place and install a matt-black ply-wood sheet to the rear surface of the mesh. From the outside, an observer sees only the mesh. Make sure there is disguised access from the living compartment to the driver's seat. It should look like there is no access from the driver's compartment to the cargo space behind. On the back windows, use something that completely blocks the light, but can be easily removed if desired. Avoid fabric curtains, these scream camper-van.

Nothing valuable inside. Avoid creating the impression that the van contains valuables that someone might try to steal in the middle of the night as you sleep inside. To create this impression, remove the radio-CD player from the dash, and anything else of value in the driver's compartment. You can always listen to your smartphone music player when driving. The driver's compartment needs to look minimalist, workman-like with no-frills. Casually place a well-used invoice book, or delivery schedule on the dash where it can be easily seen through the windscreen. Do not leave a GPS unit anywhere in sight. A well-used paper-based street directory for the current city is a convincing detail. An investigator walking around the vehicle will take note of these details and in all likelihood decide this is a harmless van. There should be nothing visible to suggest otherwise.

Active and passive security. Install a car alarm that can be manually operated. Place a discrete sticker on the driver's window or windscreen that indicates that an alarm is on duty. If you think someone is breaking in, flip the switch and sound the alarm. This will deter all but the most determined thief. Install deadlocks on the cargo doors so they cannot be opened with a pry-bar. Use a wheel lock on the steering wheel. Use lock-nuts on the wheels. Create the impression that this van would not be worth breaking into or stealing.

Keep the van clean and tidy. Keep the van in good condition in the way that a business maintains its vehicles in good, but not pristine condition. A tired, dirty vehicle looks suspicious and might even be mistaken for an abandoned vehicle.

VAN INTERIOR

Keep vehicle weight to a minimum. It might be tempting to load the van with all the comforts of home, but the van will struggle under the weight, and be slower around town. Vehicles are designed to operate within certain parameters. If you use the vehicle well-within those parameters, it will last a lot longer than one that is used at the limits of it design capabilities. A van sitting low on its suspension is more likely to attract thieves.

Separate battery. Install a second deep-cycle battery or bank of batteries that can be charged by the alternator, but isolated from the engine starter battery by a switch. The vehicle's primary battery, the one that starts the motor, *must* be isolated from the camping batteries that power the lights and ventilation etc. so that you will not be stranded with a flat battery if you happen to flatten the camping batteries. If you use only low power consumption lights and appliances, you should have enough power in your camping batteries to last you for days, even up to a week or more, without needing to start the engine and recharge. You usually won't spend that long in any one place, but it is good to have the option. Obtain a plug-in battery charger to top up your camping batteries when you have access to mains power. Some multi-story car-parks have power points that you can use for this purpose, as long as you can do so without the electrical leads being obvious. Generators should be avoided, they are noisy, expensive and a prime target for thieves. A discrete solar panel lying flat on the roof and not visible from eye-level outside can be very helpful for keeping your camping batteries charged, but like generators, these strongly indicate camper-van and should be avoided unless you can make them all-but invisible.

Use low power consumption lights and appliances. LED lights are very efficient, making older generation lights redundant in a campervan where being frugal with power consumption is important. If you fit multiple LED lights throughout the interior, complete with dimmer, you can have as much or as little light as you wish. LED's with programmable colours are available that are great for mood lighting.

Computer. If you want internet access, a laptop computer uses far less power than a desktop computer and weighs less too. They can be charged from the deep-cycle batteries via a 240 volt power inverter. For internet access, either use a wireless hotspot, and/or use the hotspot of a smartphone with a data plan sufficient for your needs. A minimum of 3G data is a must, though 4G or higher will be much preferred. With a good set up, the stealth-camper can carry on an internet-based business from the comfort and privacy of his or her van.

Television. If you want TV, and not everyone does, obtain a USB-connected TV tuner so you can watch TV on your laptop rather than needing a separate TV. This will be a more energy-efficient way to watch TV, making your camping batteries last longer. Use headphones when watching TV.

Lining/insulation. Whether being used in hot *or* cold climates, line the interior (ceiling, walls, floor) with a high-performance thermal insulation. Finish it off with a heavy-duty neutral coloured cloth lining that you will not mind living with. Wood finish looks good but weighs more; its an alternative the wood sheeting is thin enough that it does not weigh too much. At night, the metal skin of the van becomes wet with condensation on the inside. Over time, mildew/mould grows in crevices and the spores can cause respiratory illness. During the day, when parked in direct sunlight, the insulation should prevent the heat from coming through. The interior surface should be cool to the touch.

Ventilation. An efficient ventilation system is absolutely vital. You usually won't be able to have the windows open if stealth is required. At a minimum, use passive roof vents. It is highly recommended to also install one or two independently-switched, silent, 12 volt fans that draw air in at one end of the van and expel it from the other end through baffled, disguised vents. The flow rate should allow for a complete turn-over of interior air every five minutes or less. Without good ventilation, vans become "stuffy" and airless quickly in warm climates, and insufferable in hot climates. With good insulation and hi-flow induction/extraction fans, you should be able to park in the sun and be comfortable inside. Computer cooling fans can be obtained inexpensively for this purpose. These low-wattage fans are efficient, quiet and designed to work for years. One should never under-estimate the importance of good ventilation in a stealth campervan. It makes a huge difference to how comfortable you are inside your van.

Access to driver's seat from within the van. You must be able to discretely move from the sleeping/living compartment in the back to the driver's seat without leaving the vehicle. This allows you to make a discrete arrival and departure from your overnight parking place. It also allows you to drive away quickly in an emergency without exposing yourself to outside danger or scrutiny.

Furnishings. A foam rubber mattress or a next generation memory foam mattress is both light-weight and comfortable. You also need somewhere to sit comfortably. The mattress can be adapted for this by propping yourself up in bed with pillows.

Stove. At a minimum, a propane fuelled stove, or methylated spirit burner can serve to boil water and cook food. The ventilation system should be turned on when using the stove which should ideally have its own dedicated extraction van above it to gather the rising steam that would otherwise condense on the interior surfaces.

Fridges are big consumers of electricity in a campervan, although high-efficiency, low power consumption models are available – for a price! A passive cooler box with ice can keep food from spoiling for several days.

Storage. Practical storage using lidded storage bins is a cost-effective option.

Install peep holes. Obtain four fish-eye peep-holes commonly used in doors to see who is on the other side. Install these in a disguised way so they are not recognised as peep-holes from the outside. It can be frustrating and frightening to hear noises outside and not be able to investigate without drawing attention to you. Depending on what you see, you might decide to slip into the driver's seat and drive away, or sound the alarm, or stay quiet and wait for whoever is sniffing around to leave.

Alarm button. Install a car alarm that can be manually operated. If someone, or worse, a group of someones are trying to gain access to the van, first of all remain calm and decide on an escape route. Activate the alarm and observe through the peep holes whether this has deterred the intruders. There's a good chance it has deterred them. If not, leave the alarm on while you make a quick exit. Only a very determined thief will persist once they realise there is someone inside the van. A note of caution here, if the intruders turn out to be law enforcement officers, and you try to leave the scene, you will be in some trouble. Use the peep-holes to determine whether the supposed intruders are actually law enforcement officers.

WHERE TO PARK

The main rules are to *(a) hide in plain sight by blending in, (b) not stay in any one place long enough to be noticed, (c) arrive late and leave early from the place where you sleep, and (d) always listen to your instincts when they tell you it is time to leave, even if there is no apparent reason.*

Conditions will vary from place to place. Some cities will be more relaxed than others towards people sleeping in their vehicles. But if you follow the advice here and play it super-safe, it is unlikely that you will have a problem.

Smaller towns, those with populations in the thousands tend to be places where everyone knows everyone else. An unfamiliar vehicle is going to stand out and be a topic of discussion. Stealth camping in these environments is not recommended unless you get permission to park in someone's driveway or back yard for a nominal fee. Cities with populations in the hundreds of thousands, or millions are anonymous places.

Scope out three possible overnight places. Reconnoitre several possible parking sites each day, or build up a list of sites that might be suitable. Never use the same site two nights in a row, or return to the same site within two weeks. Move through your list, adding new sites as you find them, removing sites that have become risky or otherwise unsuitable.

Always park legally. Carefully read the signs that regulate the conditions of parking in any location. Many areas that are regulated during the day become free after a certain time in the evening. Make it a rule to always be parked legally from an observer's point of view. Put yourself in the position of the police or parking inspector. Do they have any reason to give you a second look?

Do not arrive too early in the evening. Spend your days and early evening doing what you enjoy. If possible use the showers at a recreation facility to get clean before going to bed. After around 9:00pm when people are starting to settle down for the night, drive to your selected sleeping site. If the first site on your list does not feel right, then trust your instinct and go to the second site, or the third. Park quietly, no revving the engine, opening and closing doors, simply glide to a halt and cut the engine. Slip into the back, make the van light-proof before turning on lights, and get ready for bed. Use headphones if watching TV. A person walking past should have no clue that you are inside the van. This means not only making no sound and showing no light, but also shifting your weight carefully as you move about so the van does not visibly rock. If the van is rocking, an observer will assume you are having sex. No good can come from that. All a passer-by to see is a generic commercial van, legally parked waiting for a new day's work in the morning. If they shine a light into the driver's compartment, all they see is a bare-bones commercial vehicle, complete with book of carbon copy delivery notes tossed carelessly on the dashboard. There is nothing of any value in sight, no radio, no CD player, no valuables of any kind.

Higher density suburban areas. Parking in a street of detached houses will draw attention to your presence because everyone knows what cars belong in that street. Strangers stand out in this environment. Higher density residential areas with apartment buildings have a greater transient population. People come and go, visit, stay overnight with friends, etcetera. A non-descript van parked in such an area should attract no attention, particularly if you arrive later in the evening and leave early in the morning before people are leaving for work.

Commercial & Industrial precincts. A generic white van is a common sight in commercial and industrial precincts. Tradesmen, couriers and delivery drivers all use them. They are often to be seen parked overnight in these areas. Find a legal parking spot on the street, not on private property if you can help it.

Shopping Malls. The best kind is those that have businesses that never close. Find a site near the edge of the group of parked cars, not out by itself and isolated, and not in the middle of the group where you are more likely to be disturbed by people's coming and going. If there are no businesses open in that shopping mall, you are more likely to have security taking a close look at you. In the United States, Wal-Mart allow overnight parking.

Entertainment precincts. Cinema complexes, hotels, clubs, restaurants and amusement arcades are increasingly being grouped into entertainment precincts. Often these adjoin a large shopping mall. Look for a precinct where there are businesses that are still open after midnight. These complexes are so large and complicated that with a little searching, a safe parking place can be found.

Casinos are normally open 24 hours a day and have subsidised food on offer, plus other inducements to get people to come in and gamble. Personally, I avoid gambling, but I do not mind enjoying the subsidised facilities.

Motels. A busy motel will have guests coming and going at all hours. The smaller, less busy motels are more likely to check your license plate against the registered guests.

Hotel & nightclub car parks. People routinely leave their cars in these car parks overnight because they have had too much to drink. A van parked overnight would not normally attract attention. However, these car parks can be risky. They are places where people routinely go to transact business or partake of recreational drugs. If these folk notice you and think you are not minding your own business, they will make life uncomfortable, not to say dangerous.

Garages. A mechanic's shop car park often has cars parked overnight, awaiting repairs or collection. As long as you leave before they open in the morning, you are unlikely to have problems.

Hospital car parks. Most hospitals never close, so parking in a discrete place towards the outer edge of the car park should present no problems for the stealth camper. The usual arrive late and leave early rule applies.

Truck stops. Overnight parking at truck stops is usually permitted, even encouraged, though they can be noisy with big rigs coming and going all night. Truck stops have a range of amenities for the traveller, like showers, that can make life more comfortable. Some truck stops are like small towns, with shopping malls, food courts, entertainment precincts, even brothels. All of that in addition to facilities to make mechanical repairs to your vehicle. These mega truck stops are like airports, a self-contained, slightly surreal place that is dedicated to transience and transport. Truck stops are the lowest-risk overnight parking option.

Out of town options. I'm dealing with urban and suburban stealth camping in this book, but occasionally you'll find yourself out of town, perhaps in transit to the next town.

Highway lay-bys. The rules vary from place to place. If overnight parking is prohibited, it will clearly say so. The police simply want to prevent such places becoming camping grounds, so they will move along anyone staying there for more than a few hours. It is worth remembering that a lone vehicle parked in a dark lay-by in the middle of the night is a prime target for violent thieves.

Campgrounds. For a leisurely and completely legal stay, camping grounds are a good option. These might be stand alone or part of a National Park or State Reserve.

AVOIDING TROUBLE & STAYING SAFE

Attitude towards law enforcement. It is understandable if some stealth campers do not like the police. They have probably had less than enjoyable experiences with them in the past. If you are to remain unnoticed by law enforcement though, you must cultivate a positive attitude towards them. Why? Because our attitudes are reflected in our body language, something we can not fully disguise. Law enforcement officers are trained to notice people's body language, particularly what it looks like when a person is feeling guilty. An experienced officer will notice such a person in a crowd in a moment. It's what they do.

You are no threat to society. Regardless of your current attitude towards law enforcement, it is important to look calm and relaxed when in their presence or under CTV observation (which these days is just about anywhere in the urban environment). Your body language should say that you are relaxed and no threat to society.

Not appearing weak. There is a fine line to be drawn here. While on the one hand, you need to appear harmless, on the other hand if you go too far in that direction you become vulnerable to attack from those who would prey on the weak. The solution is to project a sense of calm confidence and strength. There is psychology to this that most of us learn in the school playground in order to survive. When people look at you, they should see someone who has good will towards the world and is not aggressive, but if attacked is more than capable of defending themselves and inflicting significant damage to their attacker. That is where the line should be drawn if you want to stay out of trouble and keep a low profile.

Carrying money. Being alone in isolated urban environments is not without risk. Bearing in mind the advice given in the *Not appearing weak* section, the best way to manage the risk of financial loss is to have a decoy wallet with a hundred dollars/euros/pounds/whatever in small bills, and a non-functioning credit card or two that you can reluctantly hand over in the event of a robbery. I devised this strategy when working as a taxi-driver on the night-shift and it works well for drug-crazed addicts who see the colour of your money and cannot wait to get away and get what they need. A second strategy is to have a debit card for everyday use that you periodically transfer funds to. Stored value MasterCard and Visa cards are easy to obtain from supermarkets, newsagents etc. Do not carry your Automatic Teller Machine card with you. Instead, keep it somewhere safe, either in a well-concealed place in the van, or somewhere else like a secure storage locker. The overall strategy is to limit the amount you can lose at any one time to something affordable.

Should I carry a weapon? Law enforcement considers the carrying of weapons like baseball bats, hand-guns and knives a very serious matter, even if you have a license for the gun and claim it is purely for self-protection.

They do not know what you might be using these deadly weapons for. Plus, the old saying is very true that if you pull a gun (or a knife) on someone, you had better be prepared to use it, because if you don't they will likely take it from you and use it against you. Even a baseball bat can be considered a dangerous offensive weapon. The best kind of weapon is something (like a steering wheel lock, or wheel brace) that has a lawful place in your vehicle that can be redeployed if necessary as a defensive weapon. Pepper spray is also a useful defensive weapon that can be easily explained as such, and which can come in very handy if someone is breaking into your van.

CONCLUSION

These are the basics of living the stealth camper life. It outlines what you need to do to setup, live and stay safe living a low-cost life-style in urban and suburban areas.

Beyond this, you are free to go about living your life, on or off the grid, in whatever way you choose. It is all about being free to live how you want.

Good luck to you!

PART 2: ENJOYING SOLITUDE

Van life will be for many a solitary life. At a practical level, the limited amount of space will make having a second person living with you difficult.

But people who choose this life will often be those who are by nature introverts who prefer their own company and enjoy solitude.

This bonus section has been made available with kind permission of **Altiora Publications**, from the book Being Alone by Dr. David Tuffley. I am very grateful to Altiora and Dr Tuffley as this this material can be of great benefit to the stealth van dweller. It describes how to create a good state of mind living alone. It shows you how to build a state of mind that turns the negative experience of loneliness into the positive experience of solitude.

ONE: THE BASICS

There is a dynamic tension within all of us. It is created by the competing needs for solitude on the one hand, and for company on the other. We all have these competing needs, though the degree differs between individuals. Extraverts will need the company of others more than an introvert.

Sometimes we are able to get the balance right. Other times not so much; we might feel the need to be alone when we in company and of course times when we are alone and crave company.

We cannot change this aspect of human nature. It is hard-wired into us at a fundamental level. What we *can* do is learn live with it in a satisfying way.

LONELINESS & SOLITUDE

There is a world of difference between *loneliness* and *solitude*.

Solitude is when you are alone, but not feeling lonely; not sad, not depressed. It is a positive state of mind in which you are experiencing some aspect of your inner life. This introspection can lead to intuitive insights about yourself or your life that can be rewarding, even inspiring.

Loneliness, on the other hand, is a state of painful social isolation in which you might *want* to be in the company of others, but for a variety of reasons are not.

Remember, what you experience when you are by yourself is something *you* control, or at least have the capability to control once you learn how. It really depends on your attitude, on how you are thinking about the situation. As Shakespeare's Hamlet wisely observed; *there is nothing either good or bad but thinking makes it so.*

INTROVERTS & EXTRAVERTS

The concept of introversion-extraversion will be familiar to many. The terms have come into common usage over the years, since Carl Jung popularised them in the early 20th Century. Extraverts tend to be outgoing, talkative, and energetic. They get their energy through interacting with others. Introverts are likely to be reserved, disinclined to talk, preferring solitude to company much of the time. They get their energy from within. Contact with others is over-stimulating and leads to emotional exhaustion.

When we look around in the world, it is obvious that we are not all the same in this regard. People on the introversion-extraversion continuum follow a bell-curve distribution, with relatively few people at both ends, and the majority positioned around the middle.

That middle ground is where the competing needs for solitude and company can be brought into some kind of balance that works for you. This is the challenge. Regardless of whether you feel yourself to be an extreme introvert or extravert, there are benefits in moving to the middle ground. As a general rule, doing anything to extremes leads to a counter-reaction. Life becomes like a swinging pendulum.

Put an introvert and an extravert in the same situation and they will experience that situation quite differently. So it is necessary to simply say, if you feel that you need more company than you are having and you cannot simply go and find it, then you need a strategy for feeling better about that situation.

LONELINESS & DEPRESSION

There is a well-documented link between *chronic* loneliness and depression. Without the coping strategies to handle being alone, it is likely that depression will become a problem at some point in the future.

This section discusses the symptoms of depression. If you can recognise yourself in these symptoms, it really is time to take positive action.

You know that you are depressed when a growing sense of apathy seems to be engulfing you like a fog on all sides. You find yourself losing interest in the things you used to enjoy doing. With disturbed sleep patterns and an inability to concentrate, the situation becomes steadily worse.

Feeling this way leads to low self-esteem, making you feel worthless. Depressed people often have a love-hate relationship with food; either eating too much or too little.

It is no surprise then that depression is a leading cause of suicide. When allowed to go to extremes over time, a person naturally loses interest in continuing with a life that holds no satisfaction or joy. You quite simply lose the will to live.

THE NATURE OF LONELINESS

Loneliness is not actually about being alone. It is not feeling *connected* with others. As long as you feel a sense of connection, you do not need to experience loneliness, even though you may not be in the physical company of others.

In human societies and in primate societies too, the need to feel connected to a community exerts a powerful influence on behaviour. Society makes rules about how we must behave if we are to be accepted as members of the community. When a person breaks the rules, one of the worst punishments is social ostracism, to be isolated against your will. The only thing worse is to be executed.

Neuroscience has mapped the activity in people's brains when they are engaged in various activities. It has been clearly shown that when people cooperate with each other on a worthwhile task, the 'reward' centre of the brain is activated. It makes us feel happy, gives us a sense of satisfaction and well-being to have that feeling of connection with others.

The so-called 'mirror neurones' in our brain make it possible for us to empathise with others; to put ourselves in their shoes and experience what they are experiencing.

In an evolutionary sense, it is quite possible that our need to send, receive and process increasingly complex social information is what drove the expansion of our brains. The need for social inclusion was the driving force. Our cerebral cortex grew larger which allowed us to think logically, to understand the concept of time and also to imagine alternate realities.

Social rejection is experienced in the same way as strong physical pain. The same centres in the brain light-up in the scanners for both emotional and physical pain. Being excluded from the group in the evolutionary environment meant almost certain death, since early humans were only able to survive through being part of a cooperative group, that you could properly call a mutual protection society. Women and children were particularly vulnerable, but nobody was immune.

Psychologists today are coming to regard loneliness as being a signal that tells us we need to *reconnect*. In the past, that would be to re-join our extended family group. In the 21st Century, the options for finding meaningful connection are many, far more than were available to our ancestors.

Since the experience of loneliness has its origins in our far-distant evolutionary past, the key to transforming loneliness into enjoyable solitude might also be found in evolutionary psychology.

The sections that follow outline how to adapt our lifestyle to more closely resemble the environment of evolutionary adaptedness (the name scientists call the time and place where humans first lived).

SENSE OF PURPOSE

It would be difficult to overstate the overall importance of having a clear, strong sense of purpose in life. We are talking about the informing principle that guides your life, gets you out of bed in the morning, puts a spring in your step and fills you with enthusiasm at the thought of the day ahead.

A lonely, depressed person does not have this energising sense of purpose, this tonic that is an effective treatment for loneliness.

Let us look at what is involved in generating this sense of purpose in you.

The first step in transforming loneliness is to accept the necessity of having a strong sense of purpose.

Loneliness is essentially about needing to feel connected, and the key to cultivating this is to find a cause that you consider to be more important than yourself, and devoting some of your time and energy to it. It is essentially about transcending the egoic self in order to discover a larger sense of self in the service of a greater good of the community. It sounds counter-intuitive that being selfless leads to happiness, but it is unquestionably true, having been proven many times across cultures. As the philosopher Daniel Dennett observed, true happiness is *finding something more important than yourself and devoting your life to it.*

The Irish playwright George Bernard Shaw put it more bluntly:

"This is the true joy in life, the being used for a purpose recognized by yourself as a mighty one; the being a force of nature instead of a feverish, selfish little clod of ailments and grievances complaining that the world will not devote itself to making you happy.

I am of the opinion that my life belongs to the whole community, and as long as I live it is my privilege to do for it whatever I can.

I want to be thoroughly used up when I die, for the harder I work the more I live. I rejoice in life for its own sake. Life is no "brief candle" for me. It is a sort of splendid torch which I have got hold of for the moment, and I want to make it burn as brightly as possible before handing it on to future generations."

IN THE PAST

In the evolutionary environment, our purpose in life was simple; to survive long enough to reproduce. In today's complex, highly differentiated world, there is a bewildering array of possibilities which makes it harder to even recognise the greater good, let alone live it.

For many, the greater good is still to look after their family or to contribute in a positive way to the welfare of their community. For some, it is to work in the interests of their employer, or take up a cause for the benefit of their nation, or the whole world.

But what if you do not really know what your purpose in life is? What if your life gives you little or no satisfaction? You dislike your job or not having a job but you do it because you need the money.

Here are some practical ways to help you recognise your purpose in life.

BE HONEST WITH YOURSELF

By practicing radical honesty, your inner awareness expands and new vistas in life open up. Lack of honesty makes it easy to hold on to false beliefs or comfortable delusions. It reduces your ability to know what is real in your world. But honesty comes at a price. There will be difficult issues to sort through, and possibly negative consequences in your outer world. People often do not react well to the truth. But these consequences are relatively short-lived while the benefits are long-lived. It is a price worth paying. Honesty with yourself allows you to *be* yourself, and by extension you allow those around you to be who they are too.

Being honest requires courage and determination to rid oneself of delusion and face up to the truth, even when it is unpleasant. Many of the problems that life throws our way, particularly the recurring ones, are there because they are necessary for our overall personal growth. They will keep coming until you face them honestly and find resolution. If you refuse to accept the reality of these problems and try to side-step them, you are setting yourself up for the same problems to occur later on. Those problems will keep coming at you until you deal with them.

Finding the courage to face your fears is really the only way to defeat them and to live free. It will not be easy, but it *will* be worth it. A sense of purpose can be discerned in this spacious inner world that the truth has created, or perhaps revealed what has always been there.

When you are being honest with yourself, your purpose in life will become apparent, though it may take time, and it cannot be rushed.

Your purpose in life will be indicated by what your talents are; those abilities that you have that other people have to a lesser extent. Make a thoughtful inventory of your abilities, writing them down in a list. You might be surprised at what finds its way onto the list.

The Myers-Briggs personality test (several good free ones available online, use Google to find) is a good starting point for understanding your personality type. Apart from a wealth of personality traits, MB will give you a list of typical occupations and pastimes that people with your personality type are suited for.

Finding your purpose in life is like a launched torpedo with a guidance system that tells it when it has gone too far to one side or the other. You zero in on your target until you arrive. Your likes and dislikes guide you towards your goal in the same way.

COMPASSION

Compassion is the opposite of anger and hate. It is a virtue that benefits you in a multitude of ways. Compassion helps you find your purpose by allowing you to empathise with people and to know what their needs are.

Compassion is another name for unconditional love. It creates in you an awareness of the interconnectedness of yourself with everything in Nature, a tremendously powerful realisation. From this awareness, a sense of purpose emerges.

Allowing the opposite of compassion (anger and hate) to be your prevailing emotional state alienates you from the world. Nothing is more conducive to feeling lonely than to be angry at the world.

An angry person can be in the midst of a large crowd and feel a profound loneliness, while a compassionate person can be alone on a mountain top and despite their isolation can feel a great love and sense of connection with all humanity.

MINDFUL AWARENESS

Paying attention to your stream of consciousness over time will reveal what is important to you. Mindfulness is present moment awareness; it is an acknowledgement of one of the ultimate truths in life that the present moment is the only time we can experience life fully. When your mind is in the past or future, you are exercising your imagination. It is not real, it only exists in your head.

KNOW THYSELF

Ask yourself *who am I, what am I, what is good and what is bad for me, where am I going, what is my mission in life?* Opening yourself up in this way means recognising where your defences and blockages are -- and then finding the courage to give them up. The opposite of this is the uncritical mind-set of the person who cruises along through life, making choices based on comfort and security and the conventional wisdom of the society in which they live. They do not know themselves; they are only aware of what the outside world thinks.

Ultimately, finding your purpose in life is about asking yourself the question every day until the truth dawns.

COMMUNITY

In an ideal world we would all have strong bonds of love and friendship with a small group of special people. This group would be located within a larger community with which you have an enduring sense of connection. In the evolutionary environment, that was the optimum condition.

It may not work out that way for people living in the industrialised world of the 21st Century. The simple farming life of our ancestors has been replaced by life in crowded urban environments, with millions or tens of millions of people crowding around, most of whom you do not know and will probably never know.

While this life has the potential to be anxiety-producing, there are still many opportunities to find meaningful connection with others. Cities and towns have a multitude of formal and informal networks that you can connect with and get a sense of community. These networks exist in both physical and virtual space.

SENSE OF IDENTITY

Membership of a community contributes greatly to your sense of identity. When you feel a sense of belonging, you care about the welfare of the community and are likely to voluntarily contribute to its welfare. A powerful satisfaction comes from this that gives you a strong sense of well-being.

People in communities construct their identity based on their place and role in the community. The interests of the group will often take precedence over self-interest. You are expected to 'take one for the team' on occasion.

GEMEINSCHAFT & GESELLSCHAFT

The idea of community is expressed well by the German concept of *Gemeinschaft*. Society on the other hand is a larger entity, a structured regulated environment within which people and communities live. Then there is *Gesellschaft* which means society. Communities exist within the larger context of society.

Early humans evolved the need to belong to a community as a survival strategy. With no government welfare, extended families which largely made up communities were a support network with a *'together we stand, divided we fall'* attitude. A lone individual in the wilderness was unlikely to survive long enough to reproduce. Natural selection has favoured those who had a strong need to belong to a community.

The extended family is the earliest and perhaps the best example of a community, but community can also be based on shared place or religious belief. In today's connected world, communities can be dispersed across the entire planet. What matters is having a shared set of values or interests that unifies them as a coherent group.

For example, on the Japanese island of Okinawa where long-life is common, people form mutual support communities (called *moais*) that encourage healthy behaviour. It is human nature that we become like the people we associate with. We unconsciously learn and re-enact the behaviour that we see around us, so it is good to associate with people that we like and admire. We should avoid bad company simply for the sake of having company.

Belonging to a faith-based community is a source of great comfort and strength to many people, particularly as they get older. With church attendance dropping in the Western world, the suggestion to become part of a religious community is not likely to be welcomed, and indeed it is not for everyone.

ONE LAST THING

If you enjoyed this book or found it useful I'd be very grateful if you'd post a short review on Amazon. Your support really does make a difference and I read all the reviews personally so I can get your feedback and make this book even better.

Thanks again for your support!

Notes

_____

_____

_____

Notes

Notes

Notes

Notes

Notes

Notes

_____

_____

_____

_____

_____

_____

_____

_____

_____

_____

_____

_____

_____

_____

_____

_____

_____

_____